elementa

teacher's resource book

Innovations

a course in natural English

Morgan Lewis

THOMSON
™

United Kingdom • United States • Australia • Canada • Mexico • Singapore • Spain

Innovations Elementary
Teacher's Resource Book
Morgan Lewis

Publisher: *Christopher Wenger*
Project Manager: *Howard Middle / HM ELT Services*
Director of Product Development: *Anita Raducanu*
Director of Product Marketing: *Amy Mabley*
ELT Editorial Manager: *David Baker*
Intl. Marketing Manager: *Ian Martin*
Editor: *Lisa Darrand*

Associate Marketing Manager: *Laura Needham*
Compositor: *Process ELT (www.process-elt.com)*
Production Management: *Process ELT*
Illustrator: *Bill Pandos*
Cover/Text Designer: *Studio Image & Photographic Art (www.studio-image.com)*
Printer: *Canale*

Printed in Italy.
1 2 3 4 5 6 7 8 9 10 09 08 07 06 05

For permission to use material from this text or product, submit a request online at: www.thomsonrights.com

Any additional questions about permissions can be submitted by email to thomsonrights@thomson.com

For more information, contact Thomson Learning, High Holborn House, 50/51 Bedford Row, London WC1R 4LR United Kingdom or Thomson ELT, 25 Thomson Place, Boston, Massachusetts 02210 USA. You can visit our website at elt.thomson.com.

ISBN: 1-4130-1270-1

Contents

3

	Photocopiable	Activity	Time	Objective	Language
Unit 13 What time is it? **64**	13A What time does the post office open?	Whole class	15	To revise asking and answering about opening times, and start and finish times	*What time does the _____ open / close?*
	13B Let's go home	Pair or group work	15	To practise making suggestions, and agreeing / disagreeing	*Let's … , Me to. / Me neither, etc.*
Unit 14 Can you help me? **68**	14A Can you help me?	Group work	15	To practise making requests	*Can you / Could you … , please?*
	14B Helped by a stranger	Pair work	25	To practise describing events in the past	*The car broke down, A man came to help, etc.*
Unit 15 What're you doing this weekend? **72**	15A I might wash the car	Pair or group work	15	To revise language from **15 What are you doing this weekend?**	*I might … , It depends … , etc. Time expressions*
	15B What're you doing on Friday night?	Whole class	15	To revise future plans and degrees of certainty	*What're you doing on Friday night? I might … , etc.*
Unit 16 Are you OK? **76**	16A Are you OK?	Group work	15	To practise talking about being unwell / in pain	*I've got a cold, I feel sick, I've hurt my … , etc.*
	16B My best holiday ever	Pair work	15	To practise talking about holidays	*Where did you go? What was the hotel like?*
Unit 17 Are you ready to order? **80**	17A *Food, glorious food*	Pair work	15	To practise talking about food	*Is it a vegetable? Lettuce, rice, pasta, etc.*
	17B I'll have a coffee, please	Pair work	10–15	To practise using *I'll have …*	*I'll have a … , please. Ice and lemon?*
Unit 18 Do you sell … ? **84**	18A Shopping habits	Whole class	10–15	To practise asking questions and talking about shopping habits	*Do you buy a newspaper everyday?*
	18B Can I pay by credit card?	Pair or group work	10	To revise and extend shopping expressions	*Where's the shoe department? It's on the second floor.*
Unit 19 Sorry I can't come **92**	19A Find someone who …	Whole class	15	To practise using modal verbs	*Can you drive? I couldn't get to sleep last night, etc.*
	19B I'm sorry, I can't	Group work	15	To practice asking for help and giving excuses	*Could you carry my suitcase for me? Sorry, I've got a bad back.*
Unit 20 Do you like sport? **96**	20A Sporting pictionary	Group or whole class	15–20	To revise and sports vocabulary	*Racket, goal, net, rugby ball, golf club, etc.*
	20B Well played!	Group work	15	To practise sports vocabulary	*You forgot your football boots, The tennis courts are closed, etc.*
Unit 21 What day are you travelling? **100**	21A The longest flight	Pair work	15	To practise talking about experiences	*Present perfect Superlatives*
	21B Conversation dictation	Pair work	10–15	To practise language from **21 What day are you travelling?**	*Does this bus go to Trafalgar Square?*
Unit 22 What's she like? **104**	22A My brother's really lazy	Group work	15–20	To revise talking about character	*Character adjectives*
	22B I met Ozzy Osbourne once	Group work	15	To practise describing background information	*Past continuous*
Unit 23 What a great flat? **108**	23A I live in a block of flats	Whole class	15–20	To revise language from **23 What a great flat!**	*Huge living room, block of flats, etc.*
	23B What a lovely shirt!	Whole class	15	To practise giving compliments	*I love your trousers!*
Unit 24 Are you doing anything to celebrate? **112**	24A I don't know what to give her	Group work	15	To practise making suggestions	*Why don't you buy her some perfume?*
	24B Party time	Group work	15	To practise making suggestions and plans	*Why don't we order some pizzas? How about 9 o'clock etc?*

Introduction

Introduction

The first book in the *Innovations* series was originally created to provide intermediate to high-intermediate students with interesting models of natural spoken English to motivate them beyond the intermediate plateau. *Innovations* has now been expanded into a full series (*Elementary, Pre-Intermediate, Intermediate, Upper-Intermediate* – with the *Advanced* level in preparation) for teachers looking for a fresh approach to teaching young adult and adult students. It is based on a language-rich, lexical/grammatical syllabus that starts with the kinds of conversations that learners want to have.

Innovations Elementary Teacher's Resource Book has been designed to closely support the material in the Coursebook. The photocopiable activities build on and recycle key language from the Coursebook, while at the same time provide ways to help students develop oral fluency. Additionally, these activities allow the teacher to vary the pace and mood of the class and bring some fun and humour into the lesson.

Organisation

Innovations Elementary Teacher's Resource Book contains twenty-four units, one for each unit of the Coursebook. There are two photocopiable activities in every unit. The first activity, (*10A Have you been to Buckingham Palace?*, *19A Find someone who ...*, etc.) is more controlled and is useful for providing further practice for key lexical and grammatical items from the Coursebook. Typical activities include information gaps, card games and short, controlled mini-conversations. The second activity, (*9B I'd like to run a marathon one day*, *15A I might wash the car*, etc.) is usually freer and provides students with a basis to extend their practice of language related to the theme of the corresponding Coursebook unit. Typical activities include role-plays, interviews and discussions.

Each activity consists of *Teaching notes* and a photocopiable activity. The *Teaching notes* contain information about the activity *type, time, objective, language* and *preparation* required for it. Under *Procedure*, there are step-by-step guidelines for setting up the activity and using it with a class. An answer key is given when necessary.

There is also a suggested *Follow-up* activity, which can be given to the class as a whole or to individual pairs or groups if they finish ahead of time.

How to use the activities

Before doing an activity with a class, it is often useful to model how you want it to work. In a pair-work activity, for example, you can demonstrate with one student while the rest of the class listens. Where an activity is a game, it is a good idea to choose one group to start playing while the rest of the class gathers around to watch. It's important that you deal with any questions or misunderstandings before students go off and play in their individual groups.

Useful lexis has been included in the teaching notes under *Procedure* or in the activity sheets in special *Useful expression* boxes. However, it's a good idea to add to this when appropriate. Write phrases and collocations on the board and practise the pronunciation / sentence stress before starting the activity.

While students are doing the activity, go around and monitor their performance. You can note down examples or errors and gaps in student's vocabulary. It's also nice to note down a few examples of phrases and collocations that your students have successfully produced. You can then use these notes for a short feedback session after the activity. Write examples of appropriate language on the board and have students record them in their notebooks.

When to use the activities

There are several options for when to use these activities. Some activities can be used as an immediate follow-up to a particular section from the Coursebook. For example, you can do *3A What do you do?* or *3B I'm a hairdresser* after you have done **1 Using vocabulary: What do you do?** on page 16 of the Coursebook. Activities like *11B Take the first on the left* and *24B party time* can be used to wrap up at the end of the unit. They could also be used as a review in the next class session or even a couple of days later when the class is working through the next unit of the Coursebook.
You may select useful activities from previous units and repeat them with the class when time allows. Repeating activities is an excellent way of recycling language at later stages.

Activity types and class dynamics

There are activity types for different group dynamics, including pair work, small group and whole class activities. Some activities involve the whole class moving around, talking to different people, (*10B It's got some fantastic beaches*, *15B What are you doing on Friday night?*, etc.), while others require students to sit around a table or on the floor playing a game, (*11A Getting from A to B*, *22A My brother's really lazy*, etc.).

Depending on the make-up of your class and the set-up of the classroom, these activities can provide opportunities for students to meet and work with other students, not only those that they normally sit next to. Some of the whole-class activities encourage students to mingle and find new activity partners, (*4B What are you doing tonight?* *8B Me too, Me neither*, etc.). Doing these activities systematically will create a strong feeling of teamwork and will give learners a real sense of achievement.

Teaching notes

Activity

Whole class

Time

10 minutes

Objective

To practise asking and spelling people's names

Language

What's your name / surname?

Preparation

Photocopy and cut out the activity sheet on page 7, so there is one name card and one name form for each student.

Procedure

1. Write the following model dialogue on the board:
   A: *Hello. I'm John. What's your name?*
   B: *Carol. Hi.*
   A: *What's your surname?*
   B: *Baxter. What's yours?*
   A: *Morris.*
   B: *How do you spell 'Morris'?*
   A: *M-O-R-R-I-S.*

2. Give each student one name form and one name card. If this is a new class, ask students to write their first name and surname on their card, (but not their middle names for the moment). If the students already know each other, get them to use names of famous people instead.

3. Demonstrate the activity: using one of the name cards, say to a student: *Hello. I'm Peter. What's your name?* Elicit a reply from the student and continue the conversation based on the model on the board. Get students to complete their name form with the missing names by asking each other the questions on the board. Go around the class monitoring students' progress, making sure that students check the spelling of names.

Follow-up

Students add their middle name to their name cards – if they don't have a middle name, they can make one up. Get students to mingle, asking: *Do you have a middle name?* and adding the names to their name form. As before, students should ask each other to spell their middle names.

1A What's your surname?

First name

....

Middle name

....

Surname

....

- ✂

First name	First name ....
Middle name	Middle name ....
Surname	Surname ....
First name	First name ....
Middle name	Middle name ....
Surname	Surname ....
First name	First name ....
Middle name	Middle name ....
Surname	Surname ....
First name	First name ....
Middle name	Middle name ....
Surname	Surname ....
First name	First name ....
Middle name	Middle name ....
Surname	Surname ....
First name	First name ....
Middle name	Middle name ....
Surname	Surname ....
First name	First name ....
Middle name	Middle name ....
Surname	Surname ....
First name	First name ....
Middle name	Middle name ....
Surname	Surname ....

Teaching notes

Activity

Pair work

Time

10 minutes

Objective

To practise introducing people

Language

This is my best friend, Anna. I've known her since I was twelve, etc.

Preparation

Photocopy and cut out one complete set of cards on page 9 for each pair of students. Take care not to mix up the Student A cards with the Student B cards.

Procedure

1. Put students into pairs. Give Student A his / her cards and Student B his / hers cards.

2   Ask students to work alone to match their description cards to their picture cards. Go around the class, monitoring students' progress.

3. When everyone has finished, get students to take it in turns to introduce the people in the pictures to their partner. Elicit one or two full sentences from the prompts on the cards, so students understand what they have to do.

Follow-up

Ask students if they have any photos of family or friends to show to the class and tell the class a little bit about them. Alternatively, ask students to bring photos to the next class and do the follow-up activity as a review and a warm-up at the beginning of the next lesson.

Student A

Person: my younger sister, Katie
Age: 14
Information:
I sometimes help her with her homework.

Person: my friend, Robert
Age: 23
Information:
studies at the same university as me

Person: my professor at university
Age: about 48
Information:
a very good teacher

Student B

Person: my neighbour, Arthur
Age: 84
Information:
lives alone, wife died three years ago

Person: my best friend, Anna
Age: 24
Information:
known her since I was 12

Person: my boss, Linda
Age: about 45
Information:
very nice to work with

Teaching notes

Activity

Whole class

Time

10 minutes

Objective

To revise asking where people are from

Language

Where are you from?

Preparation

Photocopy and cut out enough cards from page 11 so there is one card for each student.

Procedure

1. Write the following on the board:
   A: *Where are you from?*
   B: *France.*
   A: *Oh really? Whereabouts?*
   B: *Liseux. In the north. It's about an hour and a half from Paris.*

2. Give each student a card. Make sure that two students in the class have the same card, (one card on the activity sheet is duplicated). If you have a large class and have made more than one copy of the activity sheet, you might have two pairs of students with the same cards.

3. Demonstrate the activity. Ask a student: *Where are you from?* Get the student to answer with the information on his / her card and continue the conversation based on the model dialogue on the board.

4. Explain to students that they should move around the room practising the dialogue on the board and try to find someone from the same place. Only two students will find another person from the same place, (unless you have given more than two students the same card).

Follow-up

In pairs, students write out dialogues based on their two cards. Students can then practise reading the dialogues together.

Italy
Monza
(in the north,
near Milan)

Spain
Tarragona
(about 1 hour
from Barcelona)

Germany
Potsdam
(about 1 hour
from Berlin)

Japan
Tokyo
(the capital)

USA
Burlington
(about three hours
from Washington)

Scotland
Livingstone
(near Edinburgh)

France
Nice
(in the south,
near Monaco)

Brazil
San Diego
(near Sao Paulo)

Argentina
Buenos Aires
(the capital)

Russia
St Petersburg
(the second city)

New Zealand
Christchurch
(on South Island)

Japan
Tokyo
(the capital)

South Korea
Pusan
(in the south)

Poland
Lodz
(about 3 hours
from Warsaw)

Turkey
Ankara
(the capital)

Teaching notes

Activity

Pair to group work

Time

10–15 minutes

Objective

To practise describing where you live

Language

It's a small town / big city, There's / There isn't a lot to do, etc.

Preparation

Photocopy and cut out one complete set of cards from the bottom of the page for each pair or small group.

Procedure

1. Give a set of cards to each pair or small group. Get students to spread the cards out face down on the table.

2. One student turns over two cards. If the two cards make a pair of opposites, (for example, *It's a big city. – It's a small town)*, the student keeps those two cards. If the cards do not make a pair, the cards are replaced face down and the next student takes a turn. The student with the most pairs at the end of the activity is the winner.

Follow-up

In pairs, get students to discuss which of the cards describe where they live. Help students with extra vocabulary that they might need.

It's in the north.	It's in the south.
It's in the east.	It's in the west.
The public transport is excellent.	The public transport is really bad.
It's quite clean.	It's quite dirty.
It's very noisy.	It's very quiet.
It's a big city.	It's a small town.
It's very modern.	It's quite old.
It gets very hot.	It gets very cold.
There's a lot to do.	There isn't much to do.

Teaching notes

Activity

Group work

Time

15 minutes

Objective

To revise talking about jobs

Language

Where do you work? I work for … ,
The money's good / bad, etc.

Preparation

Photocopy and cut out one complete set of question cards and one complete set of answer cards on page 14 for each group of three or four students.

Procedure

1. Put students in groups of three or four. Explain to students that they are going to play a game about jobs. Give each group a set of answer cards to share out equally. Then give each group a pile of question cards, face down on the table.

2. Explain the rules of the game:
- One student turns over the top question card and reads it. Students check to see if they have an answer to match. If so, he / she should say *Me* and read out his / her answer. If the answer is correct, he / she keeps the question card and reads out the next card.
- The game continues until all the cards have been matched. The winner is the student with the most questions cards at the end of the game.

Follow-up

Put the students in pairs with the question and answer cards they collected during the game. Using their cards, the pair writes a short dialogue. For example:
A: *What do you do?*
B: *I'm a nurse.*
A: *Oh, right. Where do you work?*
B: *In the hospital.*

Encourage students to develop their conversation as much as possible. Students can then practise their dialogues together.

Question cards

What do you do?	Are you the boss?	Do you like the people you work with?
What do you do?	Are you the boss?	Do you like the people you work with?
Where do you work?	Is it a good place to work?	Is it far from your house to where you work?
Where do you work?	Is it a good place to work?	Is it far from your house to where you work?

Answer cards

I'm an accountant.	Yes, I am, actually!	No, I'm not, unfortunately!
I work for a large bank.	Yes. I really like it.	Yes. Everyone is really friendly.
In the town centre.	No, not really. It's a bit boring.	Yes. It's two hours by car.
In the High Street.	Yes, they're really nice.	No. It's only ten minutes on foot.

3B I'm a hairdresser

Teaching notes

Activity

Whole class

Time

15 minutes

Objective

To practise talking about jobs

Language

What do you do? I'm a ... , I work in the centre of town, It's very interesting, etc.

Preparation

Photocopy and cut out enough role cards on page 16 so there is one for each student.

Procedure

1. Give each student a role card. Explain that they are going to ask each other what they do, using the information on the card. Allow students 2–3 minutes to read their card. Resolve any unknown vocabulary.

2. While students are reading, write the following model dialogue on the board:
   A: *What do you do?*
   B: *I'm an accountant.*
   A: *Oh, right. Where do you work?*
   B: *In an office near here.*
   A: *Do you like it?*
   B: *Yes. It's interesting work and the money's quite good.*

3. Demonstrate the activity. Ask a student: *What do you do?* Then follow the model dialogue on the board.

4. Get students to interact and ask each other in order to find out the information on the card.

Follow-up

As a class, ask students what they can remember about their classmates' jobs in the role-play. Ask:
What does Mario do?
Where does he work?
Does he like it? etc.

Hairdresser

- centre of town
- meet lots of nice people
- money not very good

Graphic artist

- design company in London
- good money
- long hours

Lifeguard

- swimming pool near here
- very boring
- money not very good

Work in a casino

- 5-star hotel in town
- quite interesting
- long hours

Dentist

- surgery near here
- very interesting
- very good money

Work for insurance company

- office about 10 minutes from here
- long hours
- boss horrible

Shop assistant

- shop in the shopping centre
- nice people
- very boring
- quite tiring

Freelance writer

- at home
- write for magazines
- very interesting
- good money

Architect

- office in London
- interesting
- good money
- but long train journey

Cleaner

- different offices in town
- very boring
- money terrible

Physiotherapist

- hospital
- very interesting
- meet lots of people
- good money

Electrician

- self-employed
- OK
- very good money

4A It sounds good

Teaching notes

Activity

Group work

Time

10 minutes

Objective

To practise discussing near future plans

Language

It sounds good, I don't really like that kind of thing, etc.

Preparation

Photocopy and cut out one complete set of cards on page 18 for each group of three or four students.

Procedure

1. Write the following on the board:
   What're you doing this weekend?
   It sounds good / interesting / boring / too expensive.
   I really like / don't really like that kind of thing.

2. Put students into groups of 3 or 4. Give each group a set of cards.

3. Demonstrate the activity:

- Elicit: *What're you doing this weekend?* from the board. Mime one of the activities on the cards and get students to try to guess what it is. When students have guessed it, show them the card and write the full sentence on the board. For example: *zoo – I'm going (to go) to the zoo.*

- Elicit a response from the board to your weekend plans, for example: *It sounds interesting*, etc.

- In their groups, students pick an individual and ask him / her: *What're you doing this weekend?* The student picks up a card and mimes the weekend plan. When someone in the group guesses correctly, the student with the card shows it to the group and they respond with: *It sounds good.* etc.

Follow-up

Still in their groups, ask students to look at each picture and discuss whether they have the activities / places in their home town.

zoo

bowling

beach

funfair

cinema

swimming pool

nightclub

circus

classical concert

football match

karaoke bar

windsurfing

4B What're you doing tonight?

Teaching notes

Activity
Whole class

Time
15 minutes

Objective
To practise talking about plans and inviting people

Language
I'm going to go for a walk, do you want to come?

Preparation
Photocopy and cut out enough cards on page 20 so there is one card for each student.

Procedure

1. Write the following on the board:
   A: *What're you doing tonight?*
   B: *I'm going (to go) swimming. What about you?*
   A: *Oh, nothing much.*
   B: *Do you want to come with me?*
   A: *Yes, OK. Swimming sounds good, thanks.*
   OR *Thanks, but I don't really like swimming.*

2. Give each student a card. Explain that they should find someone to go out with tonight. Some students already have plans, some do not. Students can make plans or change their original plan to a new one. Students have to fill in their cards with their plans or change of plans.

3. Get students to interact and use the model dialogue on the board to practise talking about their plans. Students should write their plans on their cards.

Follow-up

Ask individual students: *What're you doing tonight?* They should answer with the information on their cards. Who has the most interesting plan?

Your plan: go swimming
With ....
New plan? ....

Your plan: go shopping
With ....
New plan? ....

Your plan: go to a bookshop
With ....
New plan? ....

Your plan: nothing
New plan? ....

Your plan: play squash
With ....
New plan? ....

Your plan: nothing
New plan? ....

Your plan: go for a coffee
With ....
New plan? ....

Your plan: nothing
New plan? ....

Your plan: go for a drink
With ....
New plan? ....

Your plan: nothing
New plan? ....

Your plan: go clubbing
With ....
New plan? ....

Your plan: nothing
New plan? ....

5A When was the last time you ... ?

Teaching notes

Activity

Pair work

Time

10–15 minutes

Objective

To practise using the past simple with time expressions

Language

- *I bought a CD last week.*
- Time expressions: *yesterday, last night, at the weekend,* etc.

Preparation

Make one copy of the activity sheet on page 22 for each student.

Procedure

1. Put students into pairs. Give each student an activity sheet to fill in.

2. Demonstrate the activity. Ask a student: *When was the last time you bought a CD?* and record their answer on your activity sheet. Point out the time expressions in the box. Students should use this language to help them complete the activity sheet. Help students where necessary with vocabulary.

3. Get students to take it in turns to ask each other questions and complete the activity sheet with their partner's answers. Students should also note down whether their partner's answer surprise them or not. Go round the class and make sure students are forming questions using the correct tense.

Follow-up

As a class, ask students about the surprises they noted from their partner's answers. For example, *The last time Claudia spoke to her parents was 6 months ago.* Find out which student recorded the longest and shortest time for each item.

When was the last time you ...	When?	Surprised? (Yes / No)
(buy) a CD?		
(speak) to your parents?		
(cook) a meal?		
(wash) your hair?		
(watch) a DVD or a video?		
(write) a letter?		
(go) to the cinema?		
(take) an exam?		
(do) some housework?		
(get) takeaway food?		

Useful expressions

... a couple of hours ago.
... this morning.
... last night.
... yesterday.
... a couple of days ago.
... at the weekend.
... a couple of weeks ago.
... about a month ago.
... about a year ago.

Teaching notes

Activity

Pair work

Time

15 minutes

Objective

To revise language from **5 Did you have a nice weekend?**

Language

*   Past simple
*   Verb–noun collocations

Preparation

Photocopy and cut out one Student A card and one Student B card from page 24 for each pair of students.

Answers

Student A

I stayed **at home**.
I watched **TV**.
I went **swimming**.
I read **the paper**.
I did **my homework**.
I listened **to my new CD**.
I washed **my hair**.
I phoned **my brother**.

Student B

I went **to bed early**.
I sent **a few emails**.
I **cleaned my flat**.
I played **tennis**.
I bought **a couple of books**.
I met **some friends**.
I cooked **for some friends**.
I had **a piano lesson**.

Procedure

1. Put students in pairs. Give one student Card A and the other Card B. Explain to students that they each have halves of sentences; their partner has the other halves. Students have to match their halves.

2. One student should read out a sentence starter. The other should find the appropriate ending. Both students then record the missing information on their cards. Go around the class monitoring students' progress. If class time is short, you could make this a competition to see which pair completes the activity first.

3. When students have completed the activity, check the answers as a class.

Follow-up

In pairs, get students to test each other's memory by reading the endings and seeing if their partner can remember the collocation without looking at the activity sheet. For example:
Student A: *Swimming*
Student B: *I went swimming.*

Student A

I stayed ....
I watched ....
I went ....
I read ....
I did ....
I listened ....
I washed ....
I phoned ....
.... a couple of books.
.... to bed early.
.... a piano lesson.
....a few e-mails.
.... my flat.
.... tennis.
.... for some friends.
.... some friends.

✂ <--

Student B

I went ....
I sent ....
I cleaned ....
I played ....
I bought ....
I met ....
I cooked ....
I had ....
.... swimming.
.... to my new CD.
.... at home.
.... my hair.
.... TV.
.... my homework.
...................................my brother.
....................................the paper.

Teaching notes

Activity

Pair work

Time

10–15 minutes

Objective

To revise and extend the names of courses / academic subjects

Language

Music, economics, biology, business, etc.

Preparation

Make one copy of the activity sheet on page 26 for each pair of students.

Answers

Crossword

1	M**U**SIC
2	ECO**N**OMICS
3	B **I** OLOGY
4	**V**ETERINARY SCIENCE
5	BUSIN**E**SS
6	AG**R**ICULTURE
7	TOURI**S**M
8	CHEM **I** STRY
9	MA**T**HS
10	PH**Y**SICS

Follow-up

music
economics
biology
veterinary science
business
agriculture
tourism
chemistry
maths
physics

Procedure

1. Put students in pairs. Give one student Crossword A and the other student Crossword B. Pre-teach any unknown vocabulary needed for this activity.

2. Explain to students that they both have the same crossword but with different bits of information missing. Tell students to help each other guess the missing words by giving each other clues. Students aren't allowed to say the word itself. For example, *You learn about money and markets* (ECONOMICS). Give students a few minutes to prepare on their own before they start. Provide help with vocabulary or encourage students to use dictionaries With weaker classes, allow students to give their dues in their own language.

3. At the end of the activity, students they can check if their answers are correct because the letters in the shaded boxes should spell the word, UNIVERSITY.

   If class time is short, you could make this a competition to see which pair finishes first.

Follow-up

Write the following on the board:
Physics sounds interesting / boring / hard / good.

In pairs, students discuss the ten subjects using the structure. Ask students to write the ten subjects from the main activity in their notebooks and mark the main stress in each word. Practise the pronunciation together.

Crossword A

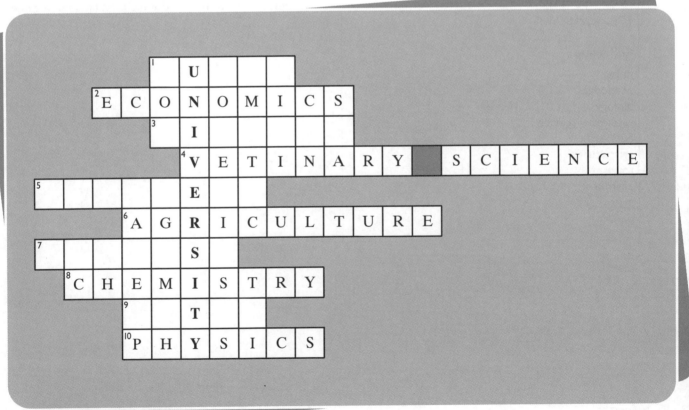

```
 1 M  U  S  I  C
 2       N
 3       B  I  O  L  O  G  Y
 4       V
 5 B  U  S  I  N  E  S  S
 6             R
 7 T  O  U  R  I  S  M
 8             I
 9          M  A  T  H  S
10             Y
```

Crossword B

```
 1          U
 2 E  C  O  N  O  M  I  C  S
 3          I
 4          V  E  T  I  N  A  R  Y     S  C  I  E  N  C  E
 5          E
 6       A  G  R  I  C  U  L  T  U  R  E
 7       R
 8 C  H  E  M  I  S  T  R  Y
 9          T
10 P  H  Y  S  I  C  S
```

Teaching notes

Activity

Group work

Time

15–20 minutes

Objectives

- To revise vocabulary of everyday objects
- To practise spelling out words

Language

What's the word for this? How do you spell that?

Preparation

Photocopy and cut out one complete set of cards from the bottom of the page for each group of four or five students.

■ Procedure

1. Pre-teach any unknown vocabulary. Then put students into groups of four or five and give each group a pile of picture cards, face down on the table.

2. Write the following on the board: *What's the word for this?* and *How do you spell it?* Demonstrate the activity. Pick up a card and show it to the class. Ask: *What's the word for this?* If a student gives you the correct word, ask: *How do you spell it?* Write the word on the board as the student spells it out.

3. In their groups, students take turns to pick up a card and ask: *What's the word for this?* If nobody knows the word, the group can ask you or use a dictionary. If anyone needs to know the spelling, they should ask: *How do you spell it?*

Follow-up

Pictionary! Give a student in each group a word written on a piece of paper, (each group gets the same word). Without speaking, the student should draw the word and the others in their group have to guess what it is.

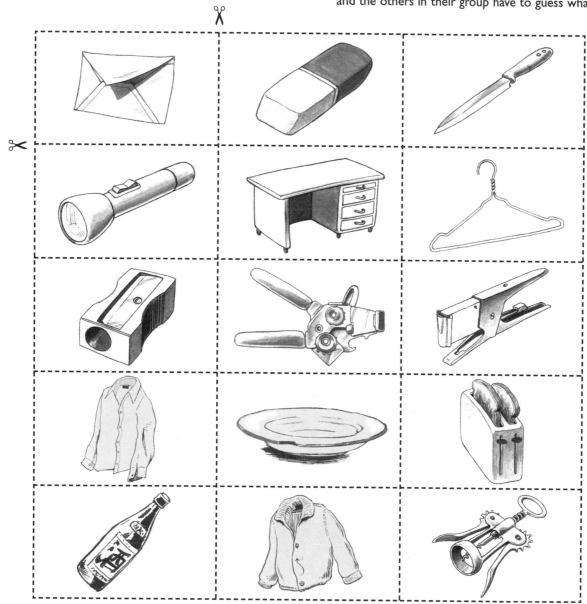

Teaching notes

Activity
Group work

Time
15 minutes

Objective
To revise the language from **7 What did you do last night?**

Language
*   *How often do you do that?*
*   Time expressions

Preparation
Photocopy and cut out one complete set of cards on page 29 for each group of three or four students.

Procedure

1. Put students into groups of three or four.

2. Write the following on the board:
    What did you do last night?
    How often do you do that?
    How long've you been doing that?

3. Give each group a set of cards in a pile, face down on the table. Demonstrate the activity. Ask a confident student: *What did you do last night?* The student turns over the top card and answers with the information on the card, using the correct verb form. Then ask the remaining two questions from the board and elicit answers from the prompts on the cards.

4. Students take it in turns in their groups to pick up a card and answer the questions.

Follow-up
Repeat the activity, but instead of students reading out the activity on the cards, they should mime the activity. The other students in their group guess the activity and then ask the follow-up questions as before.

(go) to the gym
three times a week,
not long —
about a month

(go) to church
every week,
not long —
about six months

(play) pool
every Saturday night,
quite a long time —
about ten years

(have) a driving lesson
once or twice a week,
not long —
about a month

(play) ice hockey
once a week,
not very long —
about three months

(go) to my chess club
once or twice a month,
not long —
about nine months

(go) to my salsa class
twice a week,
not long —
about two months

(go) out on my
skateboard two or three
times a week,
two or three years

(go) to my Tai Chi class
once a week,
quite a long time —
about a year

(have) my piano lesson
once a week,
quite a long time —
about four years

(play) table tennis
once or twice a week,
quite a long time —
about six years

(go) out for a run
three or four times
a week,
about three years

Teaching notes

Activity
Group work

Time
10–15 minutes

Objective
To practise talking about favourite things

Language
What's your favourite ... ?

Preparation
Photocopy one game board on page 31 for each group of three or four students. You will also need a dice and a set of counters for each group.

Procedure

1. Put students in groups of three or four and give each group a playing board and a dice, and a counter for each student.

2. Students begin on the *Start* square and take turns to roll the dice. When they land on a square, they should answer the question: *What's your favourite ... ?* relating to the subject on that square. Get students to say as much as they can about their favourite thing and give reasons for liking it. Encourage other students in the group to ask the player questions too. The turn then moves to the next player. If a player lands on the same square later, they can choose to pass or roll the dice again. Finish the game when you feel all students have had enough time to talk and enjoy the game.

Follow-up
Students choose one item that they talked about in their group and write about it in about fifty words.

start	hobby	food	actor
film			car
drink			season
country			animal
sport			colour
TV programme	month	book	weather

What's your favourite ...?

Teaching notes

Activity

Group work

Time

15 minutes

Objective

To revise language from **8 Do you like ... ?**

Language

Indian food's OK, but I prefer Chinese food.

Preparation

Photocopy and cut out one complete set of cards on page 33 for each group of three or four students.

Procedure

1. Write the following on the board:
    Tennis is OK, but I _____ squash.
    Elicit the missing word *prefer*.

2. Put students into groups of three or four. Give each pair or group a set of grey cards and a set of white cards. Tell students to spread out the sets of cards face down on the table in two sets, taking care not to mix up grey cards with white ones; the grey cards are the beginnings of sentences and the white cards are the ending prompts.

3. Explain the rules of the game:

    *   Students take turns to pick up one card from each set and read them out to the group. If the two cards make a sentence, the student keeps the cards and the turn moves to the next student in the group. If the two cards do not make a sentence then the cards are replaced and the turn passes to the next student.

    *   The game finishes when all the cards have been matched. The student with the most correct pairs of cards is the winner.

Follow-up

1. In the same small groups, students look at the pairs of cards together and say whether they agree with the statements. For example:
    A: *Red wine is OK, but I prefer white.*
    B: *Yes, me too.*
    A: *I prefer red. / I don't like wine at all.*

2. You can also revise comparative structures using some of these sentences. Write some of the sentences on the board and a comparative adjective after them and ask students to make a new sentence. For example:
    BMWs are OK, but I prefer Mercedes.
    (good) BMWs are better than Mercedes.
    Strawberries are OK, but I prefer raspberries.
    (nice) Strawberries are nicer than raspberries.

Indian food's OK, but	Chinese food	Red wine's OK, but
white wine	Classical music's OK, but	Jazz
Dark chocolate's OK, but	milk chocolate	Skiing's OK, but
snowboarding	Long hair's OK, but	short hair
BMWs are OK, but	Mercedes	Strawberries are OK, but
raspberries	Glasses are OK, but	contact lenses
Cats are OK, but	dogs	Cities are OK, but
the countryside	North France is OK, but	the south

8B Me too, me neither

Teaching notes

Activity
Whole class

Time
15 minutes

Objective
To practise talking about likes and dislikes

Language
Do you like … ? I like … , Me too. / Me neither.

Preparation
Make one copy of the activity sheet on page 35 for each student.

Procedure

1. Give each student an activity sheet. Look at the list together and resolve any unknown vocabulary. Get students to tick whether they like each item on their own. They can choose from three categories: *Yes, Not really* and *No*. Give students three minutes to complete this part of the activity.

2. Demonstrate the activity with a confident student. Say: *I like dogs.* Elicit the reply: *Me too. / Me neither.* Or: *Do you like dogs?* Student replies: *Yes, I do. / No, not really.*
According to whether the student's answer is the same as your answer on the activity sheet, write his / her name in the *Same* or *Different* column.

3. Get students to mingle. Students ask each other: *Do you like … ?* for the items in the list. For each item, students should find someone who has the same opinion as them as well as someone who has a different opinion, and write their name on the activity sheet. Go around the class monitoring students' progress, making sure students use *Me too* and *Me neither.*

Follow-up
Write on the board: *Why don't you like … ?* Find a student who doesn't like vegetables. Ask: *Why don't you like vegetables?* and elicit a reply. Students then work in pairs and ask each other: *Why don't you like … ?* for the items on the activity sheets that students don't like.

Do you like ... ?				Same	Different
Dogs?	Yes ☐	Not really ☐	No ☐		
Spicy food?	Yes ☐	Not really ☐	No ☐		
Snow?	Yes ☐	Not really ☐	No ☐		
Very hot weather?	Yes ☐	Not really ☐	No ☐		
Whisky?	Yes ☐	Not really ☐	No ☐		
Cooking?	Yes ☐	Not really ☐	No ☐		
Clubbing?	Yes ☐	Not really ☐	No ☐		
Classical music?	Yes ☐	Not really ☐	No ☐		
Cats?	Yes ☐	Not really ☐	No ☐		
Dancing?	Yes ☐	Not really ☐	No ☐		

Teaching notes

Activity

Pair or group work

Time

15 minutes

Objective

To practise using *I need to …*

Language

Cash, stamps, chemist, florist, flowers, toothpaste, etc.

Preparation

Photocopy and cut out one complete set of cards on page 37 for each pair or group of three or four students.

Procedure

1. Pre-teach any unknown vocabulary needed for this activity.

2. Divide the class into pairs, or groups of three or four students. Each group needs a set of item cards (grey) and a set of place cards (white). Students share out the item cards equally among themselves and put the pile of place cards face down on the table.

3. Explain the rules of the game:
   - A student turns over the top place card.
   - Students look at their item cards to see if they have a card that matches the place card, for example, *tennis balls – sports shop.* The student with the matching card takes the place card and makes a sentence, for example: *Ah, good. I need to buy some tennis balls.*
   - The turn passes to the next student and the game continues in the same way. Go around the class monitoring students' progress. Make sure students use the correct quantifier where appropriate, (*some toothpaste, a flight,* etc.).
   - The student who matches all their item cards first is the winner.

Follow-up

Memory game: in the same groups, students put the place cards face down again in a pile. The item cards are not needed for this activity. The first student turns over the top card, for example, the *bank* card. The student has to remember the item that went with this card and make this sentence: *I went to the bank to get some cash.* The next student does the same and adds a sentence based on the card he / she turns over: *I went to the bank to get some cash, and I went to the post office to buy some stamps.* Students take turns to turn over the cards, repeat the sentences already produced and add one of their own. If students can't remember all the items in order, they must drop out of the game until there is one winner remaining.

tennis balls	sports shop
toothpaste	chemist
stamps	post office
cash	bank
flowers	florist
photocopying	photocopy shop
e-mails	internet cafe
flight	travel agent
tie	clothes shop
bread	baker's

9B I'd like to run a marathon one day

Teaching notes

Activity
Individual and group work

Time
10 minutes

Objective
To practise expressing hopes about the future

Language
- *I'd like to …*
- Time expressions

Preparation
Make one copy of the activity sheet on page 39 for each student.

Procedure

1. Pre-teach any unknown vocabulary, for example, *marathon* and *cosmetic surgery*.

2. Write the time expression *sometime in the future* on the board. Elicit similar time expressions and write them on the board. Here are some examples:
   sometime in the next year
   sometime in the next few years
   sometime in the next three or four months
   one day

3. Give each student an activity sheet. Look at the first statement, *I'd like to run a marathon*. Find out if this is true for any of the students by eliciting: *Me too*. Refer students to the expressions on the board and ask: *When would you like to do that?*

4. Allow students five minutes to complete the activity sheet alone. Then put students in pairs or groups to compare answers. Go around the class and help students to use the time expressions to develop their conversations.

Follow-up
Working as a class, ask each student to tell you one thing that someone in their group would like to do and when. For example: *Timo would like to write a book one day.*

I'd like to ...	Agree	Disagree
. . . run a marathon.		
. . . learn a musical instrument.		
. . . buy my own flat / house.		
. . . go travelling.		
. . . be famous.		
. . . write a book.		
. . . get married and have children.		
. . . live in a different country.		
. . . change jobs.		
. . . have cosmetic surgery.		

Teaching notes

Activity

Group work

Time

15–20 minutes

Objectives

To practise using *Have you been … ?*

Language

Time expressions

Preparation

Photocopy and cut out one complete set of role cards on page 41 for each group of students.

Procedure

1. Put students into groups of four. Give each student in the group a different role card.

2. Explain the activtiy:
*   Ask students to imagine the class is on a language trip to London and students want to visit as many places as possible during their stay. The information on their card tells them the places they have already visited and if they liked them or not.
*   Students should find out what places the others in their group have visited and what they thought of them.
*   The conversation in this role-play relates to the conversation, *Have you been there?* in exercise 4, page 48 of the Coursebook. You may want to play the conversation again to set the scene before you start the role-play.
*   Demonstrate the activity by asking a student: *Have you been to … ?* If the student answers: *Yes*, write in when they went and ask: *Did you like it?* and write in their answer.
*   Students now ask each other the questions for all the places and fill in the missing information. Make sure the students are asking and answering the questions, not just showing each other their role cards.

Follow-up

Find out if any students have been to any of these famous places in London. If some students have, get other students to ask follow-up questions: *When did you go?, Did you like it?, etc.* For those who have never been to London, find out what they would like to see. Revise the structures, *I'd like to …* and *It sounds … .*

Name: ....

Place	When ?	Was is good ?
Buckingham Palace	yes / yesterday	yes / really interesting
The Tower of London		
Oxford Street		
The Natural History Museum		
Madame Tussauds		

Name: ....

Place	When ?	Was is good ?
Buckingham Palace		
The Tower of London	yes / went last Saturday	bit boring
Oxford Street		
The Natural History Museum		

Name: ....

Place	When ?	Was is good ?
Buckingham Palace		
The Tower of London		
Oxford Street	yes / went last Sunday	yes / great shops / expensive
The Natural History Museum		

Name: ....

Place	When ?	Was is good ?
Buckingham Palace		
The Tower of London		
Oxford Street		
The Natural History Museum	yes / day before yesterday	amazing / recommend it

Teaching notes

Activity

Group work

Time

15 minutes

Objective

To practise using *It's got ...*

Language

Incredible scenery, lovely beaches, great parks, good golf course, etc.

Preparation

Photocopy and cut out one complete set of cards on page 43 for each group of three students.

Procedure

1. Put students into groups of three. Give each group a set of picture cards and a set of prompt cards. Students should spread out the cards face down on the table in two separate sets, taking care not to mix up the picture cards and the prompt cards. While students are doing this, write on the board: *It's got ...* and the adjectives: *very good, excellent, lovely, fantastic, beautiful, great, amazing.*

2. Explain the rules of the game:
   - Explain that students have to match the picture cards to the description cards. Explain that students take it in turns to turn over one card from each set. If the picture card and the prompt card match then the student has the opportunity to keep the cards if he / she can say a sentence relating to the cards. (Refer students to the structure and the adjectives on the board.) Hold up two matching cards and say, for example: *It's got some great sports facilities.* Ask students if they think the sentence is correct. During the game the other members in the group should decide whether students' sentences are correct.
   - If the cards don't match, the cards are replaced and the turn passes to another player.
   - Start the game. Move around the class, helping with vocabulary when necessary. The winner is the student with the most pairs when all the cards have been matched.

Follow-up

Ask students to write a short description of the best place they have ever visited. Write the following the board:
The best place I've ever visited is ...
It's got ... and it's got ...
If you go there, you should ...
Give students five to ten minutes to write their descriptions, then ask some students to read theirs to the class.

beach	gardens	golf course	wildlife
nightlife	old buildings	art galleries	shops
restaurants	walks	market	sports facilities

Teaching notes

Activity

Pair or group work

Time

15 minutes

Objective

To revise travel language from **11 Is there one near here?**

Language

Take the wrong turning, miss your train, get lost, etc.

Preparation

Photocopy one game board on page 45 for each pair or group. You will also need a counter for each student, and a dice for each pair or group.

Procedure

1. Put students in pairs or groups of three.

2. Explain the rules of the game:
*   Players start on the *Start* square.
*   Players take turns to roll the dice and move forward the number of squares shown.
*   If a player lands on a square containing a statement, he / she should read it out. If it is a positive statement, for example: *You buy a map*, the player moves forward an extra square; if it's a negative statement, the player moves back a square.
*   The game finishes when both or all players reach the *Finish* square.

Follow-up

Write the following on the board:

A: *How was your journey?*
B: *It was fine …*

A: *How was your journey?*
B: *Not very good …*

1. Elicit endings to the first response, for example, *The train was on time. Someone showed me where to go.* etc. Then elicit ways the second response could finish, *I missed the train. I got lost.* etc.

2. Put students in pairs, making sure each pair has a dice. A student asks his / her partner: *How was your journey?* The partner rolls the dice. If the number shown is even, he / she should give the positive response: *It was fine …* and complete the sentence with a positive statement from the game board. If the number shown on the dice is odd, he / she should give a negative response in the same way. Students will have to change the verb into the past tense, so move around the class helping and prompting when necessary.

50 FINISH	**49**	**48** You get on the wrong bus.	**47**	**46** You lose your map.
41	**42** The bus driver tells you when to get off.	**43**	**44** Someone gives you bad directions.	**45**
40 The taxi is really cheap.	**39**	**38** You fall asleep on the train.	**37**	**36** Someone gives you good directions.
31	**32** You miss your bus.	**33**	**34** You take the wrong turning.	**35**
30 The traffic is good.	**29**	**28** You arrive on time.	**27**	**26** You buy a map.
21	**22** The bus is on time.	**23**	**24** The traffic is terrible.	**25**
20 Your train is late.	**19**	**18** It's a beautiful day.	**17**	**16** Your car runs out of petrol.
11	**12** You get off at the wrong stop.	**13**	**14** You get lost.	**15**
10 Someone shows you where to go.	**9**	**8** You arrive late.	**7**	**6** It's raining.
1 START	**2** You find the bus stop no problem.	**3**	**4** Your bus breaks down.	**5**

Teaching notes

Activity
Group work

Time
15 minutes

Objectives
To practise giving and understanding directions

Language
Take the first on the left, Go straight across, It's on the corner, etc.

Preparation
Photocopy and cut out one set of maps on page 47 for each group of four students.

Procedure

1. Put students in groups of four. Give each student in the group a different map.

2. Write on the board: *Take the first on the left*. Elicit more directions until you have enough for students to complete the task. Draw a simple street map to help elicit the language above.

3. Explain that each student has the same map, but with their house marked on it, (A, B, C and D). Student A in each group should give directions from the school to his / her house. The other students in the group mark on the map where they think student A lives. Then student B gives directions from the school to his / her house and the other students mark the house on the map. This continues in the same way for all the students.

4. When everyone in the group has given their directions, students compare maps to check that they marked the houses in the right place.

Follow-up
Keep students in the same groups.
Write on the board:
A. Supermarket
B. Cinema
C. Newsagent
D. Chemist

Student A should mark a place on the map for a supermarket, Student B, a cinema, etc. Students should not show each other where they mark their places. Student A now gives directions from his / her house to the supermarket. The other students should mark where they believe it is. Student B gives directions from his / her house to the cinema, Student C to the newsagent, and so on.

When the last student has finished giving directions, all students can compare maps and see if they have marked the correct places on their maps.

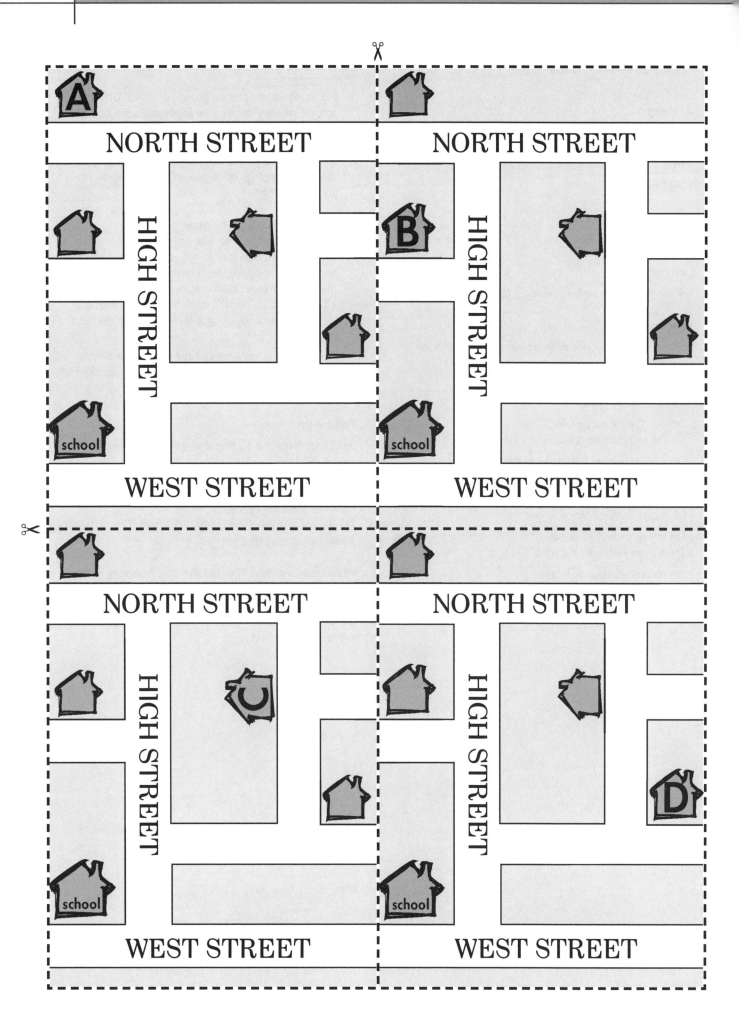

Teaching notes

Activity

Pair or group work

Time

10–15 minutes

Objective

To revise the present continuous for unfinished activities

Language

I'm not feeling very well, I'm studying Russian, etc.

Preparation

Photocopy and cut out one complete set of cards on page 49 for each pair or group of three students.

Follow-up answers

I'm not feeling very well.
Oh, I'm sorry to hear that.

I'm waiting for my friends to arrive.
How long have you been waiting?

I'm visiting my sister for the weekend.
Oh really? Whereabouts does she live?

I'm trying to find a chemist.
There's one just down the road.

I'm travelling around Europe.
Really? Which countries have you been to?

Procedure

1. Put students in pairs or groups of three. Give each pair or group a set of grey cards and a set of white cards. Tell students to spread out the sets of cards face down on the table in two sets, taking care not to mix up grey cards with white ones; the grey cards are the beginnings of sentences and the white cards are the endings.

2. Explain the rules of the game:
   - Students take turns to pick up one card from each set and read them out to the group. If the two cards make a sentence, the student keeps the cards and the turn moves to the next student in the group. If the two cards do not make a sentence then the cards are replaced and the turn passes to the next student.
   - The game finishes when all the cards have been matched. The student with the most correct pairs of cards is the winner.

Follow-up

While students are playing the game, write on the board:
Oh, I'm sorry to hear that.
How long have you been waiting?
Oh really? Whereabouts does she live?
There's one just down the road.
Really? Which countries have you been to?

When students have finished the card matching game, ask them to match the follow-up statements and questions on the board to five of the sentences from the card. You could make it a race to see which pair or group can do it first.

12A | I'm travelling around Europe

I'm not feeling	**very well.**
I'm eating	**a lot more fruit and vegetables these days.**
I'm studying	**Russian and linguistics at Oxford.**
I'm trying	**to find a chemist.**
I'm travelling	**around Europe.**
I'm visiting	**my sister for the weekend.**
I'm working	**three days a week at the moment.**
I'm thinking	**about changing jobs.**
I'm waiting	**for my friends to arrive.**
I'm spending	**too much time on the computer.**

Teaching notes

Activity

Group work

Time

20 minutes

Objective

To practise asking and answering questions

Language

Question words

Preparation

Make one copy of the questionnaire on page 51 for each student. Make enough copies of the role cards for each student in the group, (groups of four).

Answers

a. Thomas
b. Thomas
c. Angela

Procedure

1. Put students into groups of four.

2. Ask students to imagine that they are all visiting a city and they are at a party, meeting new people. Give each student a role card and an activity sheet. Explain that students should ask questions to fill in the missing information.

3. Look at the activity sheet together. Elicit the full question forms needed to ask the six questions at the top of the questionnaire and write one example on the board, for example, *How long have you been here?* Students should then read their role card. Check for any unknown words.

4. Get students to stand up and question each other in their groups. Students should continue until they have completed the questionnaire.

5. While students are interacting, write the following questions on the board:
   a. *Who has been here the longest?*
   b. *Who is staying the longest?*
   c. *Who has been here before the most times?*

6. When everyone has finished, give students a few minutes to answer the three questions. They can do this in pairs.

Follow-up

Put students in pairs and get them to ask and answer questions about the other people on their questionnaires using the third person, for example, *How long has Peter been here?* etc.

Questionnaire

	how long (you be) here?	(you be) here before?	what (you do) here?	where (you stay)?	what (you think) of it here?	when (you leave)?
Peter						
Maria						
Thomas						
Angela						

- ✂

Role Cards

Peter
- arrived two days ago – my first time here
- really like it – really interesting
- visiting my brother
- staying at brother's flat
- leaving tomorrow

Thomas
- arrived a month ago – my second time here
- like it – very friendly
- working here for three months in total
- staying in a flat near my office

Maria
- arrived here three weeks ago – my first time here
- don't like it – too busy, too noisy
- doing an English course in a language school
- leaving in one week

Angela
- arrived this morning – sixth time here
- love it – so beautiful
- visiting my boyfriend – staying with his parents
- leaving in a couple of days

Teaching notes

Activity
Whole class

Time
15 minutes

Objective
To revise asking and answering about opening times, and start and finish times

Language
What time does the _____ open / close?

Preparation
Make one copy of the activity sheet on page 53 so that there is one card for each student.

Procedure

1. Give each student a card. Explain that there is one fact they know, written at the top of the card and there are three things they need to find out. Elicit the questions and write on the board:
    post office:
    What time does the post office open / close?
    film:
    What time does the film start / finish?
    coach:
    What time does the coach arrive / leave?

2. Get students to move around the room asking each other questions until they find the person with the information they need to mark the time on their clocks.

Follow-up

Take some TV listings into class. Put students in pairs, each pair with different TV listings. They should write six questions about start and finish times of programmes. When they have finished, they swap their questions and TV listings with another pair's questions, and see who can answer all the questions first.

✂

The bank closes at 3.30 p.m. ◯

post office / close? .... ◯

supermarket / open? .... ◯

football match / start? .... ◯

The post office closes at 5.00 p.m. ◯

library / open? .... ◯

coach / leave? .... ◯

film / start? .... ◯

The supermarket opens at 8.00 a.m. ◯

film / finish? .... ◯

concert / start? .... ◯

school / open? .... ◯

The football match starts at 7.45 p.m. ◯

supermarket / open? .... ◯

film / start? .... ◯

bank / close? .... ◯

The coach leaves at 5.15 p.m. ◯

school / open? .... ◯

bank / close? .... ◯

supermarket / open? .... ◯

The film starts at 8.15 p.m. ◯

library / open .... ◯

film / finish? .... ◯

football match / start? .... ◯

The film finishes at about 11.00 p.m. ◯

concert / start? .... ◯

supermarket / open? .... ◯

coach / leave? .... ◯

The concert starts at 8.00 p.m. ◯

school / open .... ◯

film / start? .... ◯

film / finish? .... ◯

Teaching notes

Activity
Pair to group work

Time
15 minutes

Objectives
To practise making suggestions and agreeing / disagreeing

Language
Let's ... , *Me too.* / *Me neither*, etc.

Preparation
Photocopy and cut out one set of statement cards (grey) and one set of *Let's ...* cards (white) on page 55 for each pair or group of three students.

Procedure

1. Put students in pairs or groups of three. Give each pair or group a pile of statement cards face down on the table. Get students to share out the *Let's ...* cards between them.

2. Explain the rules of the game:

    •   A student picks up the top card from the pile of statement cards and reads it. For example: *I'm a bit hungry.* Students look at their *Let's ...* cards to see who has the best matching response, (*Me too. Let's get something to eat*). The student with the matching card takes the statement card.

    •   The turn passes to another student, who picks up the next statement card, reads it out, and students in the group look to see if they have the matching card.

3. The winner is the student with the most pairs when all the cards have been matched.

Follow-up

In the same pairs or groups, students write a follow-up *Let's ...* sentence for each of the dialogues on the cards. For example:
A: *I'm tired.*
B: *Me too. Let's sit down for bit.*
A: *OK. Let's sit on the grass over there.*

I'm tired.	Me too. Let's sit down for a bit.
I'm a bit hungry.	Me too. Let's get something to eat.
I need something to drink.	Me too. Let's find a pub.
I don't want to drive to Oxford.	Me neither. Let's take the train.
I don't want to go out tonight.	Me neither. Let's stay in and watch TV.
I need a new tennis racket.	Me too. Let's go to that new sports shop.
I don't understand this grammar.	Me neither. Let's ask the teacher.
I need a haircut.	Me too. Let's find a hairdresser.
I heaven't got any money.	Me neither. Let's go to the bank.
I haven't seen the new Jude Law film yet.	Me neither. Let's go and see it this weekend.

Teaching notes

Activity

Group work

Time

15 minutes

Objective

To practise making requests

Language

Can you / Could you ... , please?

Preparation

Photocopy and cut out one complete set of cards from the bottom of the page for each group of three or four students.

Procedure

1. Put students into groups of three or four. Write on the board: *Can you ... , please? Could you ... , please?*

2. Using one of the cards from the activity sheet, mime a request to the class. Encourage students to guess what the request is. When they get it, show them the card.

3. Give each a group a set of cards, face down on the table. Students take it in turns to take a card and mime the request to their group. Encourage students to use their dictionaries to resolve any unknown vocabulary. Decide how strict you want to be on students guessing the exact wording – for a strong class, you might want them to guess the exact wording to make it more challenging.

Follow-up

Put students in pairs. They write dialogues based on some of the requests they have mimed. Write an example dialogue on the board, eliciting some of the language from students as you write. For example:
A: *Could you lend me some money?*
B: *Yes, how much do you need?*
A: *Is £5 OK?*
B: *Sure. No problem.*
A: *Thanks, very much. I'll pay you back tomorrow.*

Can you pass the newspaper, please?	Could you carry my bag for me?	Could you lend me some money?	Could you give me a lift?
Can you open the door for me, please?	Could you look after my dog for me?	Could you make me a cup of coffee, please?	Can you do the shopping?
Can you help me with my homework?	Can you close the curtains, please?	Can you turn the radio up a bit, please?	Can I borrow your pullover?
Can you close the window?	Can you talk more slowly, please?	Could you repeat that, please?	Could you answer the phone for me?

14B Helped by a stranger

Teaching notes

Activity

Pair work

Time

25 minutes

Objective

To practise describing events in the past

Language

The car broke down, A man came to help, etc.

Preparation

Make one copy of the activity sheet on page 58 for each pair of students.

Procedure

1. Remind the students of the two stories on page 70 of the Coursebook, describing two people's experiences of being helped by strangers.

   Put students in pairs. Give half the pairs in the class Story A cards mixed up, and the other half Story B cards mixed up.

2. In their pairs, students put the cards in the correct order to make a story. Then, they write notes about what happened to the person in trouble, using the first person. Set a time limit for students to complete their notes. Go around the class monitoring students' progress, helping with vocabulary and encouraging use of dictionaries.

3. When students have finished, get them to join another pair with a different story to form groups of four. Get students to relate their stories to the other pair. Go around the class making sure students contribute equally.

Follow-up

Put students in pairs, each student having worked on a different story. Get students to teach each other new words and expressions that they learned while writing their stories.

Story A

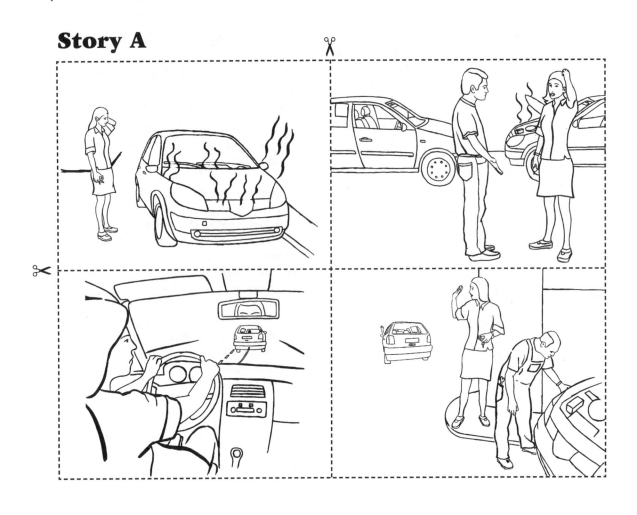

Story B

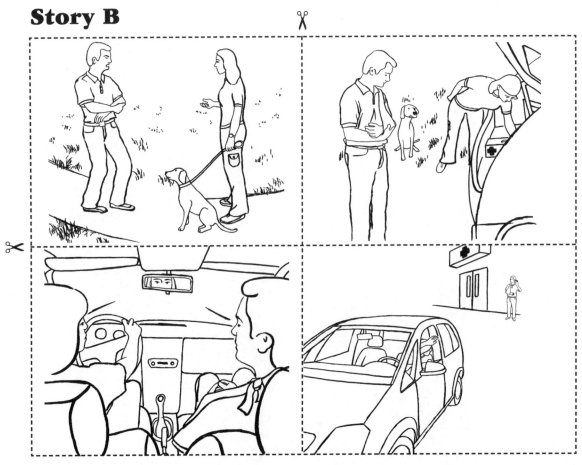

Teaching notes

Activity

Pair or group work

Time

15 minutes

Objectives

To revise language from **15 What are you doing this weekend?**

Language

* *I might ...* , *It depends ...* , etc.
* Time expressions

Preparation

Photocopy and cut out one complete set of grey and white cards on page 60 for each group of students.

Procedure

1. Write on the board:
    A: *What are you doing tomorrow?*
    B: *I'm not really sure yet. I might ...*
    A: *I haven't decided yet. I might ...*

    Elicit ways of finishing the two replies. For example, *go to the cinema, go shopping*, etc. Then write these sentences on the board and ask students to finish them:
    It depends on ... (the weather)
    It depends how ... (I feel)
    It depends if ... (I have time)

2. Put students into groups of three. Give each pair or group a set of grey cards and a set of white cards. Tell students to spread out the cards face down on the table in the two sets, taking care not to mix up grey cards with white ones; the grey cards are the beginnings of sentences and the white cards are the endings.

3. Explain the rules of the game:

* Students take turns to pick up one card from each set and read them out to the group. If the two cards make a sentence, the student should add another sentence beginning: *It depends ...* . He / She then keeps the cards and the turn moves to the next student in the group. If the two cards do not make a sentence then the cards are replaced and the turn passes to the next student.

* The game finishes when all the cards have been matched. The student with the most correct pairs of cards is the winner.

Follow-up

Ask students to write their plans for this evening on a piece of paper. Collect the pieces of paper and read the first one aloud to the class. Students have to guess which student wrote that sentence. Repeat with more pieces of paper.

the car on Sunday.	**I might wash**
I might watch	my flat tonight.
painting my bedroom tomorrow.	**I might go**
I might spend	my brother and his wife on Saturday.
the football match on TV tonight.	**I might visit**
I might just stay	at home all weekend.
shopping in London on Saturday.	**I might start**
I might cook	for same friends on Friday night.
all day in bed!	**I might tidy up**
I might play	tennis tomorrow afternoon.

Teaching notes

Activity

Whole class

Time

15 minutes

Objectives

To revise future plans and degrees of certainty

Language

What're you doing on Friday night? I might … , etc.

Preparation

Make one copy of the activity sheet on page 62 for each student.

Procedure

1. Give each student a questionnaire. Look at the sheet together and explain that students should think about their plans from Friday night to Sunday night and write in any plans they have. They may have definite plans (*I'm going to …*), probable plans (*I'll probably …*), possible plans (*I might …*), or no plans at all.

2. Elicit questions needed to ask about someone's plans and write them on the board: *What're you doing on (Friday night)? Have you got any plans for (Saturday)?* etc. Go through the *Useful expressions* box under the questionnaire and check students' comprehension.

3. Allow 5 minutes for students to fill in their questionnaire. If students do not have plans for the whole weekend, they can make some up.

4. Demonstrate the activity by asking a few students their plans for different parts of the weekend and get them to ask you, too. Use language from the *Useful expressions* box and encourage students to role-play arranging to meet up with you. Students now interact and ask each other about their plans. Encourage them to arrange to meet if they want to. Give students about 10 minutes to do this. Then discuss students' plans as a class. Are there any firm arrangements?

Follow-up

Write your weekend plans on the board, (make them up if necessary). For example:
On Friday night I'll probably just stay at home. On Saturday morning, I going to go into town to buy some shoes and in the afternoon, I might go to the beach with some friends – it depends on the weather. On Saturday night … , etc.

Students use the information from their questionnaire to write about their plans in the same way.

15B What are you doing on Friday night?

Questionnaire

When?	No plans?	I might ...	I'll probably ...	I'm going to ...
Friday night				
Saturday morning				
Saturday afternoon				
Sunday morning				
Sunday afternoon				
Sunday evening				

Useful expressions

That sounds interesting.
Why don't you come with me?
Let's meet in / at ...
What time?
I don't have any plans.
I'm not really sure yet.
It depends how I feel / on the weather / if I'm tired.

Teaching notes

Activity

Group work

Time

15 minutes

Objective

To practise talking about being unwell / in pain

Language

I've got a cold, I feel sick, I've hurt my ... , etc.

Preparation

Photocopy and cut out one complete set of cards on page 64 for each group of three or four students.

Procedure

1. Put students in groups of three or four students.

2. Demonstrate the activity: mime a headache. Get students to guess what the problem is, then write the question on the board: *Have you got a headache?* Write the following on the board:
   Have you got a ... ?
   Have you hurt your ... ?
   Have you cut your ... ?
   Do you feel ... ?

2. Give each group a set of cards, face down on the table. A student takes the top card and mimes the problem written on the card. Help students with new words or ask them to use their dictionaries. The others in the group have to guess what the problem is using the question starters written on the board. For example: *Have you got a cold? Have you hurt your leg? Do you feel sick?* The student who guesses correctly takes the next card and mimes what it says. The game finishes when all the cards have been used up.

Follow-up

Put students in pairs. Students write short dialogues based on one or two of the cards. For example:
A: *I've got a headache.*
B: *Do you want some paracetamol?*
A: *Oh, thank you. That would be great.*

A: *I've cut my finger.*
B: *Do you want a plaster?*
A: *No, it's OK. It's not too bad.*

You've hurt your back.

You've got a cold.

You feel sick.

You've cut your finger.

You've got a sore throat.

You feel faint.

You've hurt your shoulder.

You've got toothache.

You feel very tired.

You've hurt your arm.

You've got a fever.

You feel very weak.

Teaching notes

Activity

Pair work

Time

15 minutes

Objective

To practise talking about holidays

Language

Where did you go?
What was the hotel like?

Preparation

Make one copy of the activity sheet on page 66 for each student.

Answers

The full questions should be:

Where did you go?

When did you go?

What was the place like?

Did you stay in a hotel?

What was the hotel like?

What was the food like?

What was the weather like?

What were the people like?

What did you do every day?

Procedure

1. Put students in pairs and give each student an activity sheet.

2. Explain to students that they are going to talk to each other about their best holiday ever. Get students to look at their activity sheet and elicit one or two full questions from the prompts: *Where did you go? Did you stay in a hotel?* etc.

3. Get students to work together in pairs to form full questions and write them in the question column. Then students ask each other questions about their best holiday ever and write the answers in the answer column. Allow around eight minutes for this part of the activity, then ask students to describe their partner's best holiday to the class, using the third person.

Follow-up

Write on the board: *Your worst holiday ever!*
Give students five minutes to work alone and write about their worst ever holiday experience. Put students in pairs or groups of three to tell each other about their bad holiday experiences.

	Question	Answer
where / go?		
when / go?		
what / place / like?		
stay / hotel?		
what / hotel / like?		
what / food / like?		
what / weather / like?		
what / people / like?		
what / do / each day?		

Teaching notes

Activity

Pair work

Time

15 minutes

Objective

To practise talking about food

Language

*   *Is it a vegetable?*
*   *Lettuce, rice, pasta*, etc.

Preparation

Make one copy of the activity sheet on page 68 for each pair of students.

Answers

1. MUSHROOM	9. CAULIFLOWER
2. GRAPES	10. KIWI
3. SAUSAGE	11. BROCCOLI
4. SALMON	12. RICE
5. LEMON	13. TOMATO
6. PAPAYA	14. MUSSELS
7. AVOCADO	15. PASTA
8. LETTUCE	

Procedure

1. Using flashcards or pictures drawn on the board, elicit / teach any unknown food vocabulary students need to complete the activity.

2. Give each student in the pair a different crossword.

3. Explain to students that their crossword contains food words that are missing from their partner's crossword. Students have to help each other complete their crosswords by giving each other clues to the missing words, but without saying the word itself.

    Demonstrate: *Number 1: It's a kind of fruit. It's green. You don't eat the skin. It begins with the letters 'A' and 'V' (AVOCADO). Number 2. It's a vegetable. You eat it in salads. There are different kinds. It is usually green. It begins with 'L' (LETTUCE)*, etc.

    With weaker classes, allow the students to give clues in their own language.

3. Give students a few minutes on their own to prepare before they start. Help with vocabulary or encourage students to use dictionaries. Explain to students that they can check if their answers are correct because the letters in the shaded boxes make the phrase, *REALLY DELICIOUS*.

    If class time is short, you could make this a competition to see which pair finishes first.

Follow-up

Word chain game: write *mushroom* on the board. Ask students to give you another food that starts with the last letter of *mushroom*, (*melon*). Ask for something that starts with the last letter of *melon*, (*nut*). Then put students into groups of three or four and ask them to continue the chain. The group that carries on the chain the longest is the winner.

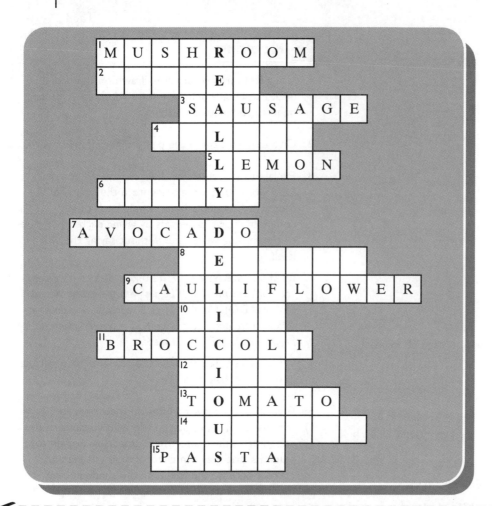

Student A

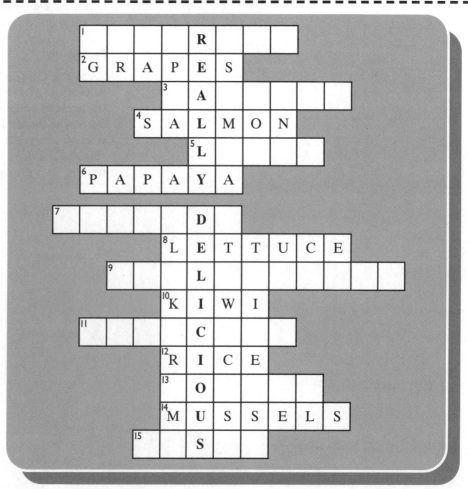

Student B

© Copyright Thomson ELT, a part of the Thomson Corporation

Teaching notes

Activity

Pair work

Time

10–15 minutes

Objective

To practise using *I'll have …*

Language

I'll have a … , please.
Ice and lemon?

Preparation

Photocopy and cut out one complete set of cards from the bottom of the page for each pair of students.

Procedure

1. Put the students in pairs and give each pair a set of cards. Ask students to spread out the cards, face down on the table.

2. Students take it in turns to turn over two cards. If a student turns over a pair, for example, *coke – ice and lemon*, he / she keeps the cards. If the two cards do not make a pair, they are replaced and the turn passes to the other student.

3. Once all the pairs have been found, students use the cards to create short dialogues. For example:
   A: *What would you like to drink?*
   B: *I'll just have a coke, please.*
   A: *Ice and lemon?*
   B: *Yes, please.*

Follow-up

Students write a slightly longer dialogue, based on a couple of pairs of cards, and then act it out for the class.

coke	Ice and lemon?
wine	Red or white?
cheeseburger and chips	Eat in or take away?
potatoes	Boiled or roast?
soup	Chicken or mushroom?
coffee	With milk or cream?
apple pie	With ice cream or custard?
ham and tomato sandwich	White or brown bread?

Teaching notes

Activity

Whole class

Time

10–15 minutes

Objectives

To revise practise asking questions and talking about shopping habits

Language

Do you buy a newspaper every day?

Preparation

Make one copy of the activity sheet from the bottom of the page for each student.

Procedure

1. Give each student an activity sheet. Look at the statements together, and ask students if they think the statements are true or false. Students write what they think in the *Your guess* column.

2. Elicit the question forms of the statements, as students will need to ask these questions in order to complete their surveys. You may want to write some of the questions on the board.

3. Get students to mingle and survey each other.

4. Now look at the statements again as a class. Allow discussion to take place then agree as a class before filling in the third column. You could finish up by asking: *Who spends the most / least on clothes? Who buys the most CDs?* etc.

Follow-up

Students work alone and try to list what they spend money on every week. Put students in pairs to compare their lists and suggest to each other ways they could spend less every week.

Are these statements true about your class?	Your guess: True or false?	Results: True or false?
At least two students hate going shopping.		
Most students buy a newspaper every day.		
At least two students spend £50 or more a month on clothes.		
At least one student buys a CD every week.		
Less than three students buy a magazine every week.		
At least one student always pays for things in cash.		
Most students have a credit card.		
At least three students go to the same shop every Saturday.		

18B Can I pay by credit card?

Teaching notes

Activity

Pair or group work

Time

10 minutes

Objectives

To revise and extend shopping expressions

Language

Where's the shoe department? It's on the second floor.

Preparation

Photocopy and cut out one complete set of grey and white cards on page 72 for each pair or group of students.

Procedure

1. Put students in pairs or groups of three. Give each pair or group a set of grey cards and a set of white cards. Tell students to spread out the sets of cards face down on the table in two sets, taking care not to mix up grey cards with white ones; the grey cards are the beginnings of sentences and the white cards are the endings.

2. Explain the rules of the game:
- Students take turns to pick up one card from each set and read them out to the group. If the two cards make a sentence, the student keeps the cards and the turn moves to the next student in the group. If the two cards do not make a sentence then the cards are replaced and the turn passes to the next student.
- The game finishes when all the cards have been matched. The student with the most correct pairs of cards is the winner.

Follow-up

In pairs, students choose one or two of the sentences from the cards and write short dialogues. For example:
Where's the shoe department?
It's on the second floor, up the escalator.
Great. Thanks.

Can I help you?
Yes. Have you got this in a medium?
I'm not sure. Let me have a look.

Students can then present their dialogues to the class.

Have you got this top	in medium?
Can I pay	by credit card?
Where can I try	this on?
Where's the shoe	department?
Do you sell	stamps?
Can I have £50	cash back, please?
I'm returning	this top. It's too small.
That's £50	altogether.
The cosmetics department is on the second	floor, up the escalator.
The football magazines are on the bottom	shelf. Can you see them?
The post office is just round	the corner.
I'll meet you outside the	main entrance.

Teaching notes

Activity

Whole class

Time

15 minutes

Objective

To practise using modal verbs

Language

Can you drive? I couldn't get to sleep last night, etc.

Preparation

Make one copy of the activity sheet on page 74 for each student.

Procedure

1. Give each student an activity sheet. Elicit the questions students need in order to complete the activity sheet. Write a few on the board if necessary:
   Can you drive?
   How many languages can you speak?
   Could you lend me £20?
   Could you swim when you were four years old?
   Did you sleep OK last night? etc.

2. Get students to mingle and ask each other questions to complete their activity sheets. Ask students to try to find a different name for each statement. Set a time limit of 10 minutes.

3. Go through the statements as a class and find out which names were written down for each statement. For some of the statements, ask students: *Why ... ?* For example: *Why couldn't you sleep last night?, Why did you have to get up early this morning?*

Follow-up

As a class, compile a bar chart on the board of the results of the activity. Discuss any surprising results with the students.

Find someone who ...	Name
... can't drive.	
... can speak three languages.	
... can't sing.	
... could lend you £20.	
... could swim when he / she was four years old.	
... couldn't sleep last night.	
... has to work this weekend.	
... sometimes has to babysit a brother or sister.	
... had to get up early this morning.	
... had to work last weekend.	

Teaching notes

Activity

Group work

Time

15 minutes

Objectives

To practise asking for help and giving excuses

Language

Could you carry my suitcase for me? Sorry, I've got a bad back.

Preparation

Photocopy and cut out one complete set of grey and white cards on page 76 for each pair or group of students.

Procedure

1. Put students into groups of three or four. Give each group a set of request cards (grey) and a set of excuse cards (white). Students should deal out the cards so that each member of the group has an equal number of request and excuse cards.

2. A student reads out one of his / her request cards to another student in the group. That student finds a suitable excuse card to reply with and reads it out to the group. The group should decide if the excuse is suitable. If it is, the student gives the excuse card to the student who made the request. If it is not suitable, the student should take the request card. (There might be disagreement at times over whether an excuse is suitable. Let the groups discuss and if necessary get them to vote.)

3. The game finishes when a student has no more cards. If class time is short, set a time limit; the student with the least cards when the time is up is the winner.

Follow-up

Put students in pairs. Write on the board: *I'm sorry, but I couldn't do my homework because ... .* Get students to think of two silly or funny excuses for not doing their homework, using the structure on the board. When students have finished they can read their excuses to the class. Class votes to find the silliest or funniest excuse.

Request cards ✂ Excuse cards

Request cards	Excuse cards
Could you help me with my homework tonight?	I'm not going out until this evening.
Could you give me a lift to the station on Wednesday?	I'm going to London this weekend to see my parents.
Could you carry my suitcase for me?	I'm taking my car to the garage tomorrow.
Could you lend me £10 until tomorrow?	I have to be at the dentist in 15 minutes.
Could you have a quick look at my computer?	I'm going to wash my hair this evening.
Could you post this letter for me?	I've got an appointment at the hospital in half an hour.
Could you get me a newspaper when you go out?	I've got a bad back.
Could you help me move my piano this afternoon?	I'm going to bed early this evening.
Could you make me a cup of tea?	I'm meeting a friend in five minutes.
Could you help me fix the toilet this evening?	I'm going out, but I'm not going near the shops.
Could you look after my dog this weekend?	My sister is coming to stay with me this weekend.
Could you babysit for us on Saturday night?	I've got no money on me at all.

Teaching notes

Activity

Group work or whole class

Time

15–20 minutes

Objectives

To revise and extend sports vocabulary

Language

Racket, goal, net, rugby ball, golf club, etc.

Preparation

Photocopy and cut out one complete set of cards on page 78 for each group of three or four students.

Procedure

1. Put students into groups of three or four.

2. Give a student in each group a card, (each group should have the same cards). Without talking, he / she should draw the item on the card, while the rest of the group tries to guess what it is. See which group gets it first! Demonstrate the activity on the board first, if necessary.

   Alternatively, this game can be played as a class. Ask a student to the front of the class. Show the student one of the cards. The student draws the object on the board and the class guesses the word. The first student who guesses correctly is the next to draw on the board.

Follow-up

Ask students to choose one item from the cards and prepare a short talk based on the object and personal experience. Allow five minutes for preparation. Go around the class monitoring students' progress. Then ask students to share their experiences. Encourage students to ask each other for extra information, for example: *Why did you stop surfing?*

tennis racket	goal (football)
snowboard	**rugby ball**
golf club	swimming goggles
table tennis bat	baseball bat
basketball net	**football pitch**
gym weights	skis
surfboard	pool table
trampoline	athletics track

Teaching notes

Activity

Group work

Time

15 minutes

Objective

To practise sports vocabulary

Language

You forgot your football boots, The tennis courts are closed, etc.

Preparation

Photocopy and cut out one game board on page 80 and one set of cards from below for each group of three students. You will also need a counter for each student, and a dice for each group.

Procedure

Explain the rules of the game:
- All players start on the *Start* square.
- The players take turns to roll the dice and move forward the number of squares shown on the dice. If a player lands on a square with a question mark, he / she picks up a card and reads it aloud. If it is a positive statement, for example: *Your new tennis racket is great*, the player moves forward an extra square. If it's a negative statement, for example: *The tennis courts are closed*, the player moves back two squares. Cards should be replaced at the bottom of the pile.
- The game finishes when all players reach the *Finish* square.

Follow-up

Put students into groups of three or four. Give students five minutes to list as many Olympic sports as they can. The group with the most sports is the winner. Ask students if they think any of the sports mentioned are perhaps not suitable for the Olympics, or if they think any new sports should become Olympic sports.

Cards

You lose all your golf balls.	Your team loses 6–0.	Your team wins 4–3.	You run your best time: 19 mins, 46 seconds.
You forget your football boots.	You want to windsurf – there's no wind.	Perfect windsurfing conditions.	You weigh yourself at the gym and you have lost 1.5 kilos.
Your bike gets a puncture.	The swimming pool is very crowded.	You get a hole-in-one in your golf match.	You receive your next belt in Karate.
The tennis courts are closed.	Your volleyball team only has five players today.	Your new tennis racket is great.	You win a table tennis tournament.
You twist your ankle running in the park.	You lose a ski on a black run.	You swim 20 lengths without stopping.	Your country wants you for the Olympic Games.

50 finish	49 ?	48	47 ?	46
41 ?	42	43 ?	44	45 ?
40	39 ?	38	37 ?	36
31 ?	32	33 ?	34	35 ?
30	29 ?	28	27 ?	26
21 ?	22	23 ?	24	25 ?
20	19 ?	18	17 ?	16
11 ?	12	13 ?	14	15 ?
10	9 ?	8	7 ?	6
1 start	2	3 ?	4	5 ?

Teaching notes

Activity

Pair work

Time

15 minutes

Objectives

To practise talking about experiences

Language

*   Present perfect
*   Superlatives

Preparation

Make one copy of the activity sheet on page 82 for each student.

Answers

1.   What's the longest flight you've ever been on?
2.   What's the shortest flight you've ever been on?
3.   What's the best flight you've ever been on?
4.   What's the worst flight you've ever been on?
5.   What's the worst airport you've ever been in?
6.   What's the longest flight you've ever had?
7.   What's the most interesting train journey you've ever been on?
8.   What's the worst train journey you've ever been on?
9.   What's the busiest train station you've ever been in?
10.   What's the longest train journey you've ever been on?

Procedure

1.   Give each student an activity sheet. Look at the first prompt as a class and elicit the full question form. Write the full question form on the board. Students work in pairs to form the remaining questions. Go around the class monitoring students' progress and helping with vocabulary.

2.   Get students to ask each other the questions and record their partner's answers.

Follow-up

Describe a plane or train experience you have had. For example:

The longest flight delay I've ever had was 28 hours. I was 17, and it was a flight from London to New York. After waiting for 8 hours, the flight was cancelled and we all had to stay in a hotel near the airport. I finally arrived in New York the next day, but my luggage didn't. It arrived three days later!

Write your story on the board. Keep it short and simple. Ask students to write about one of their experiences travelling by plane or train.

Question	Answer
1. What / long / flight / you ever be / on?	
2. What / short / flight / you ever be / on?	
3. What / good / flight / you ever be / on?	
4. What / bad / flight / you ever be / on?	
5. What / bad / airport / you ever be / in?	
6. What / long / flight delay / you ever have?	
7. What / interesting / train journey / you ever be / on?	
8. What / bad / train journey / you ever be / on?	
9. What / busy / train station / you ever be / in?	
10. What / long / train journey / you ever be / on?	

Teaching notes

Activity

Pair work

Time

10–15 minutes

Objective

To practise language from **21 What day are you travelling?**

Language

Does this bus go to Trafalgar Square?

Preparation

Make one copy of the activity sheet on page 84 for each student.

Answers

1. A: Excuse me. Does this bus **go to** Trafalgar Square?
   B: No. You **need** a 32 or a 34.
2. A: Is this the **right** bus for Camden Market?
   B: Oh, good. Can you tell me when to **get off**?
3. A: I'd like a **return** to Oxford, please.
   B: **That's** £34.99.
4. A: What time's the **next** train to Liverpool?
   B: And what time does it **get in**?
5. A: What's the **earliest** train to Southend tomorrow morning?
   B: And what's the **last** train coming back at night?
6. A: What's the **best** way to get to the airport from here?
   B: I would take the train. It's really **easy**.
7. A: Excuse me. Can I get a taxi **near** here?
   B: Yes, there's a taxi rank just **round** the corner.

Procedure

1. Put students in pairs. Give each student an activity sheet. Give students five minutes to read the conversations and think about what the missing words might be.

2. Read out the missing words below, pausing for about five seconds after each one to give students time to decide where it goes and to write the word in the missing space: *right; near; need; get off; return; go to; round; next; get in; that's; last; earliest; way; easy.*

   Alternatively, for a lower level class, you may wish to read the words for each question separately:
   1   need; go to
   2   get off; right
   3   that's; ticket
   4   next; get in
   5   last; first
   6   easy; way
   7   near; round

3. Get students to compare their answers in pairs, then check the answers as a class.

Follow-up

Students practise reading the dialogues with their partner.

1. A: Excuse me. Does this bus _____ Trafalgar Square?
   B: No. You _____ a 32 or a 34.
   A: Oh, OK. Thanks.

2. A: Is this the _____ bus for Camden Market?
   B: Yes, it is.
   A: Oh, good. Can you tell me when to _____?
   B: Yes, no problem. Take a seat.

3. A: I'd like a _____ to Oxford, please.
   B: Coming back today?
   A: No, tomorrow.
   B: _____ £34.99.

4. A: What time's the _____ train to Liverpool?
   B: In fifteen minutes – the 10.47.
   A: And what time does it _____?
   B: 11:30

5. A: What's the _____ train to Southend tomorrow morning?
   B: 05:45.
   A: And what's the _____ train coming back at night?
   B: 1.30 a.m.

6. A: What's the best _____ to get to the airport from here?
   B: I would take the train. It's really _____.
   A: OK, thanks.

7. A: Excuse me. Can I get a taxi _____ here?
   B: Yes, there's a taxi rank just _____ the corner.
   A: Oh, great. Thanks.

Teaching notes

Activity

Group work

Time

15–20 minutes

Objective

To revise talking about character

Language

Character adjectives

Preparation

Photocopy one game board on page 86 for each group of three or four students. You will need a dice for each group and one counter for each student, (you can use coins).

Procedure

1. Put students into groups of three or four. Pre-teach any unknown vocabulary needed for this activity.

2. Explain the rules of the game:
   - Students may place their counters on any square.
   - The first student rolls the dice and moves the counter clockwise the number of spaces shown on the dice. The student reads the adjective on the square he / she has landed on and should think of someone they know whom the adjective describes. They should make two sentences about that person, for example: *My brother's really lazy. He never helps in the house.* The turn then passes to the next student.
   - If a player lands on the same square twice, they can roll again if they want to. Set a time limit for the game. Alternatively, have students retire from the game if they can't thing of a sentence, until there is one winning student remaining.

Follow-up

Ask students to find opposite pairs of adjectives from the board. Some are clear opposites; others are not so clear cut, so allow students to disagree a bit on some of the pairs. Let students use their dictionaries.

Possible pairs:
very cold – very friendly
very outgoing – very shy
very patient – very impatient
really lazy – really hard-working
really funny – really boring
very gentle – very aggressive

very bossy

very boring

very friendly

very dangerous

very moody

really funny

very aggressive

very patient

really impatient

really rude

very outgoing

very creative

very cold

hardworking

really fit

really lazy

a bit strange

very shy

very gentle

very clever

Teaching notes

Activity

Group work

Time

15 minutes

Objectives

To practise describing background information

Language

Past continuous

Preparation

Photocopy and cut out one complete set of cards on page 88 for each group of three or four students.

Procedure

1. Put students into groups of three or four. Give each group a pile of cards, face down on the table.

2. Write on the board: *I met _____ once* and the following questions:
   What was he / she like?
   Where were you?
   What were you doing?
   What was he / she doing?
   What was he / she like?

3. Mention a time when you saw or met someone famous. Say: *I met _____ once.* Elicit the questions on the board from students and provide model answers using the present continuous. Write some of your answers on the board too, if necessary.

4. Explain the rules of the game:
   - Students take turns to pick up a card and use the information on the card to tell the group about a time when they saw or met someone famous. Students use the information on their cards and their imagination to answer other students' questions.
   - When the conversation comes to a natural end, the turn passes to the next student in the group.

Follow-up

In the same groups, ask students to think about this question: *Which famous person would you most like to meet?* Give students a few minutes to think about their answer. When all students have thought of someone, get them to answer this question: *If you could ask that person one question, what would you ask?* Give students a few more minutes to think and write down the question they would ask. Help students where necessary. Then ask students to share their answers in their groups.

George Bush In McDonalds, buying a hamburger	*Jennifer Anniston* On a beach in Hawaii, sunbathing	*David Beckham* In London, getting into a taxi
Kylie Minogue In a shop in London, standing in the queue	*Tony Blair* At the swimming pool, getting changed	*Serena Williams* In a hotel in Tokyo, checking in
Orlando Bloom New Zealand, swimming in the sea	*Ozzie Osbourne* In the supermarket, buying some milk	*Nicole Kidman* Outside my house, talking on her phone
Tiger Woods In New York, waiting for a taxi	*Prince Charles* On a mountain in Scotland, walking his dogs	*Jude Law* At a café in London, drinking a cappuccino

3A I live in a block of flats

Teaching notes

Activity
Whole class

Time
15–20 minutes

Objective
To revise language from **23 What a great flat!**

Language
Huge living room, block of flats, etc.

Preparation
Photocopy and cut out one copy of the activity sheet on page 90 for each student.

Procedure

1. Give each student an activity sheet. Go through the activity sheet as a class. Elicit the question forms students need in order to complete the sheet, for example: *Do you have a large garden?* Help with vocabulary where necessary.

2. Students interact and ask each other the questions until they have a name for each statement. Ask students to try to find a different name for each statement.

Follow-up

Ask students to write a short description of their favourite house or flat. Perhaps write your own example on the board. For example:
My favourite house is my parents' old house. I was born there and lived there for 23 years. It was about five minutes from the sea and you could walk to the shops. It was a big house, with five bedrooms. It had a big garden with an apple tree. My favourite room was the dining room because that was where the whole family met to eat and talk.

Find someone...	Name
... who has a very large garden.	
... who lives in a block of flats.	
... who has a tiny kitchen.	
... who shares a bedroom.	
... who lives on a very busy road.	
... who has a spare bedroom.	
... who has a huge living room.	
... who has a garage.	
... whose bedroom is very small.	
... whose house / flat is very central.	
... whose house / flat is very convenient for the shops.	
... whose house / flat is over 50 years old.	

Teaching notes

Activity

Whole class

Time

15 minutes

Objective

To practise giving compliments

Language

I love your trousers!

Preparation

Photocopy and cut out enough cards on page 92 so that each student has two.

Procedure

1. Write the following on the board:
   A: *What a _____ top! It really _____ you.*
   B: *Thank you very much.*
   A: *Where did you _____ it?*
   B: *That new shop in the shopping centre.*

   Ask students to give you the missing words (*lovely / super, suits, get / buy*). Now write the following on the board:
   A: *I _____ your top!*
   B: *Thank you very much.*
   A: *How long _____?*
   B: *Oh, I bought it last week.*

   Ask students to give you the missing words (*like / love, have you had it*). Give each student two cards. (Avoid giving him / her two cards the same.)

2. Demonstrate the game: walk around the class and give a student a compliment using a card you are holding and role-play the dialogue on the board. When the conversation is finished, give your card to the student you complimented. Let students interact and give and receive compliments.

3. Monitor students' and end the activity when you think students have exchanged enough compliments.

Follow-up

Put students in pairs. Using some magazines that you have brought in or the Coursebook, students browse the pages, looking at the photographs and commenting on what people are wearing, or their hairstyles, etc. You could introduce some negative comments to use as well: *What a horrible shirt! I don't like that jacket at all. What a terrible hairstyle!* etc.

belt (interesting)	**hair** (I love …)	**trousers** (I love …)
top (lovely)	**watch** (nice)	**pen** (interesting)
belt (interesting)	**hair** (I love …)	**trousers** (I love …)
top (lovely)	**watch** (nice)	**pen** (interesting)
glasses (I love …)	**shoes** (fantastic)	**skirt** (fantastic)
bag (super)	**jacket** (great)	**boots** (I love …)
glasses (I love …)	**shoes** (fantastic)	**skirt** (fantastic)
bag (super)	**jacket** (great)	**boots** (I love …)

Teaching notes

Activity

Group work

Time

15 minutes

Objective

To practise making suggestions

Language

Why don't you buy her some perfume?

Preparation

Photocopy and cut out a set of gift cards (grey) and a set of people cards (white) on page 94 for each group of students.

Procedure

1. Put students into groups of three or four and give each group a set of gift cards and a set of people cards.
2. Get students to deal out the gift cards equally and place the people cards face down in a pile.

3. Demonstrate the game:
- Pick up a people card and say, for example: *It's my (mum's) birthday next week and I don't know what to buy her.* Get students to look at their cards and see if they have an appropriate gift suggestion. Elicit suggestions: *Why don't you buy her (some perfume)?* Reply with: *She doesn't really like (perfume).* Elicit another gift suggestion from a different student. Reply with: *That's a good idea. Thanks.* That student should then give you their gift card.
- Write the model conversation on the board:
  A: *It's my (mum's) birthday next week and I don't know what to buy her.*
  B: *Why don't you buy her (some perfume)?*
  A: *She doesn't really like (perfume)* OR: *That's a good idea. Thanks.*
- Students can now play the game in their groups. Encourage students to persuade each other that their gift ideas are the best, as the winner of the game is the first student to get rid of all their cards.

Follow-up

Give students five minutes to write answers to the following questions:
- Did you get a nice present for your last birthday? If not, did you get something you didn't like?
- What was it?
- Who gave it to you?
- How did you feel when you saw it?
- What did you say?

Students can either share their experiences in small groups or as a class.

Gift cards

a football	a razor and shaving foam	a baseball cap
flowers	a tie	a CD
a box of chocolates	some earrings	a scarf
perfume	a computer game	a mobile phone

People cards

my boss	my 12-year-old niece	my 15-year-old nephew
my grandfather	my mum	my dad
my sister	my best friend	my grandmother
my teacher	my boyfriend	my girlfriend

4B Party time

Teaching notes

Activity

Group work

Time

15 minutes

Objective

To practise making suggestions and plans

Language

Why don't we order some pizzas? How about 9 o'clock? etc.

Preparation

Photocopy and cut out one complete set of cards on page 96 for each group of students.

Procedure

1. Put students into groups of three or four.

2. Explain to the groups that they are going to organise a party, (if you are near the end of your course, you could call it the end of course party). The group members should decide together what kind of party they want and plan the details.
   Write the following on the board:
   Why don't we / you … ?
   How about … ?
   Let's …
   OK, I'll …

3. Elicit ways to finish the sentences. For example: *Why don't you organise the food? How about getting a DJ? Let's invite the other classes. OK, I'll ask them*, etc.

4. Give each group a set of cards face down on the table. Appoint a student in each group to take notes. One student turns over the top card and reads the question. Together, the group should decide what they want to do. The note-taker makes a note of their decision. They then turn over the second card and continue in the same way until they have done all nine cards. Go around the class monitoring students' progress.

   Write the following on the board:
   We're going to …
   We're thinking of …
   Give the groups five minutes to review their decisions from their notes and write down their plans using the two sentence starters above.

5. Finish by asking someone from each group to tell the class what their plans are.

Follow-up

The best idea would be to have a party!

Which night of the week? Friday? Saturday? Other?	Where will it be? The school? Someone's house? A pub?	**What time will it start? And finish?**
Will there be food and drink? *Who will prepare it?* *Who will pay?*	Will there be music? What kind? How will you do it?	Who will you invite? Just your class? The whole school? Friends and family? Invitations?
Dress code? *Smart?* *Casual?* *Fancy dress?*	**Will there be any special entertainment? Speeches? Games? Prizes?**	Who will be in charge of: The food and drink? The music? The entertainment? Any other important jobs?